PUPPETS AT LARGE

Puppets as partners in learning and teaching in the Early Years

By Linda Bentley
Foreword by Jenny Mosley

LEARNING THROUGH PUPPETS

To Emma and Jessica - for all their love.

Acknowledgements

Throughout the writing of this book, I have been fortunate to have a wonderful team of people supporting me every step of the way. This remarkable mix of family members, friends, work colleagues and professional associates were unfailing in their respective roles: offering advice and encouragement to enable me to keep forging ahead. Finally, my deepest thanks go to my husband, Martin, for his endless practical and emotional support - from beginning to end.

Published in 2005 by:
Positive Press Ltd
28A Gloucester Road
Trowbridge
Wiltshire BA14 OAA

Telephone: 01225 719204
Fax: 01225 712187
Email: positivepress@jennymosley.co.uk
Web site: www.circle-time.co.uk

Reprinted 2006, 2007

Text and photographs © Linda Bentley
The puppets in this book are featured with the kind permission of 'The Puppet Company UK' and 'Living Puppets'

ISBN 1-9048660-2-6

Printed by:

HERON PRESS
19-24 White Hays North
West Wilts Trading Estate
Westbury
Wiltshire BA13 4JT

Contents

I met Linda on our in-depth, accredited Quality Circle Time course in Cornwall. My senior consultant Maggie Grayson led part of the course, flanked by two large brightly-coloured, smiling puppets and a huge photograph album she had made celebrating all their antics!

Thank you to Maureen Woodhouse, Head of Early Years, for setting up the course and supporting the initiatives that developed from it. Linda was so inspired by this course module that she set off to explore and develop all the ideas within her own practice. Building on all her own previous knowledge and dedicated years of experience working with early years children, she created a whole swathe of new ideas. Hey presto, a fabulous new book for early years practitioners was born.

Life is never that simple! It has taken Linda years to research all the ideas and test out a range of techniques and strategies. Fortunately, in her current role as an advisor with Cornwall's Early Education Team, she has the opportunity to encourage and inspire others to use puppets in their work with young children through training and demonstration sessions with a whole range of practitioners.

Practitioners trying out puppets learn that very young children can come to realise that they too can become agents of change, knowledge and hope through their conversations with the puppets. Children find that they possess the power within themselves to give solutions to problems and to ask challenging questions. They learn that it helps others when their ideas are put into effect. Through willingly suspending disbelief the quietest child can whisper words of encouragement to a shy puppet and a noisy child learns to listen carefully to catch the shy voice of a puppet.

When puppets are used, circle time becomes a time of pure engagement. Feelings are discussed, problems shared and new social skills and fun games are tried out together. A safe place is created for children to grow emotionally and socially.

It's also important that you keep the experience of using puppets safe too. We are always careful to stress, when the puppets visit children, that this is our special 'pretending time'. At the end of the sessions, we put the puppets in their special place so we can enjoy 'pretending' another day. Of course children's imagination brings the puppets alive. This is a willingly shared suspension of disbelief. We all enter the world of make believe together - but we need to be clear about stopping together. We advise practitioners not to leave puppets lying around the room. Let the puppets have their own special place. This adds crispness to the rituals of getting them out or putting them away together.

Many people say to me on my courses 'It's alright for you... I'm not really the puppet type'. I do empathise with these sentiments. Some of us genuinely find it difficult, but don't give up. Being creative with children does demand small acts of courage. Your children need to see you playing and having fun. We need to role-model a lot of joys, so that the natural laughter and wisdom of children can be released.

So thank you, Linda, for helping us towards wonderful experiences we can all explore together. This is a splendid book, which I believe will become an indispensable companion to all early years practitioners.

Jenny Mosley

Discovering the magic

"You know it's the first time I've heard these little ones laugh," she said, "I mean really laugh. There is nothing quite like that sound - when children really let go and chuckle like that. It's moments like these that make working with young children so worthwhile."

These were the words spoken to me by a play assistant following a storytelling session I had carried out in a pre-school recently. I knew what she meant and shared in her excitement. I, too, had experienced at first-hand the satisfaction gleaned from having a group of delighted three- and four-year-olds actively responding to something I had delivered to them. Quite simply, I had given them pleasure and in return they had given me their rapt attention and the sound of their laughter. This was my reward.

You might already be thinking that I am about to instruct you in some advanced technique or revolutionary educational approach. After all, engaging successfully with such young children can never be that easy! It might surprise you to discover that the storytelling session was neither innovative nor sophisticated but it did have one very special ingredient - a puppet.

You could say that the use of puppets was one of the earliest survival skills I developed as a teacher, having discovered from my first few days in front of my nursery class just how uncompromising a group of disaffected three-year-olds can be. Only comedians on the northern working men's club circuit have to face audiences that tough! If the problem was so overwhelmingly great then the answer when it came was proportionately simple; I needed to rethink my act completely if I was to seize and sustain the children's interest and ultimately get my messages across to them. They needed exciting sights and sounds and - not forgetting - surprises. And puppets are wonderful at delivering surprises!

I now know that I was not alone in feeling anxious during my first experiences in Early Years education. From time to time as I travel around pre-schools and nurseries in my advisory capacity today, I sometimes come across a despondent practitioner who confesses to dread or even actively avoids the session's group story time, complaining that their young children 'just won't sit and listen'. The common conclusion among such practitioners is that the children are too young.

My response is to ask them to reflect upon any occasion where they have observed children of this age as they gaze, fully absorbed, at the television screen while one of their favourite animated characters recounts a story. There isn't a problem with either the sitting still or the listening then, is there? The route to success, as with so many other aspects of your work, lies not so much in what you do, but the way in which you do it. Let's go back to the beginning of the chapter, to my reflection on the puppet and storytelling session at the pre-school. I believe that the children's laughter was an expression of their surprise - their delight at witnessing the unexpected. Professor Timothy Brighouse talks about 'surprising kids into learning' and believes good teachers 'weave magic' into their teaching. By being entertaining, it is possible to consolidate the learning you work so hard to achieve.

Learning and teaching are what Early Years practitioners are all about, so it makes sense to use whatever helps you to make that happen. By bringing puppets or other toys to life, you suddenly have the ability to do something bigger and better than you could do on your own. Puppets capture children's imagination and help you to challenge the boundaries of their understanding.

Why practitioners need puppets

What is it about these characters that makes them such a valuable aid to children's learning? Primarily, they are so versatile. With a little imagination, you can use them to help you deliver high quality learning experiences for children across the whole Foundation Stage curriculum. This book includes a chapter offering practical ideas to help you achieve this in your own setting.

Puppets are particularly effective in fostering and developing a child's social and emotional development. The QCA's Curriculum Guidance for the Foundation Stage underlines the crucial importance of developing a child's competence in this area of learning: 'Successful personal, social and emotional development is critical for very young children in all aspects of their lives and gives them the best possible chance of success in all other areas of learning'.

Because puppets are essentially non-threatening they are wonderful for helping you to raise and explore sensitive issues with children and they can actually help bring about the bonding process between a child and the practitioner or carer. The importance of establishing this trust cannot be over-stressed although the process can present real challenges. Some children struggle to take those essential early steps and it is up to you to find ways to help them overcome this. Puppets can often help to bridge that gap, allowing satisfactory attachments to form and thereby offering vulnerable children the support they need.

The sheer excitement and sense of anticipation which a puppet generates is almost enough to convince even the most reluctant practitioner to have a go. After all, you probably chose to work with this particular age group because you enjoy the uninhibited feedback you have come to expect from the children and you have learned to take pleasure in the things that delight them too.

There can be no doubt that you cannot always predict the response you will generate when you dabble in this form of magic - but getting a response is a positive sign that you are doing something right! Perhaps it is this feeling of being slightly out of control that deters some adults from getting involved with puppets. Personally, I get a real buzz from it; the secret is to be prepared for the unexpected!

Children today live in a world of sensual overload. They are a generation of emotionally and culturally abandoned children whose bedrooms resemble hi-tech entertainment centres, even at an early age. They are often starved of the simple pleasures many of us took for granted and enjoyed as children - the storytelling, prolonged conversations with interested adults, the comfort of a shared bedtime story. They crave physical contact but many have learned to live without it. There is never a better time than now to redress this balance.

Think about your own school experience. Which teachers do you remember most? I could hazard a guess that most of you would conjure up memories of those who could deliver something slightly outlandish, something fun and 'out of the ordinary'. They were the discerning ones. They instinctively knew that the seeds of your early learning would be attached to to these memories.

Puppets provide the visual stimulus you need to entice children into the adult domain. Once you have them 'with you' then you will have little difficulty in encouraging them to really focus and develop their concentration skills. Learning suddenly becomes much more fun for everyone. "I don't do puppets!" said one particular pre-school supervisor when I approached her during a support visit some years ago. My answer to her then, remains unchanged today; "Well, it's never too late to start!"

Welcome to the magical world of puppets: let's explore it together.

Puppet preparations - a guide to getting started

Choosing your puppet

It's really not difficult to set the ball rolling as far as puppets are concerned. In fact, this is the really exciting part of the adventure. But where do you begin? Naturally enough, you need to decide on a puppet that particularly appeals to you as an adult. Whichever one you choose, it is likely that it will have the same level of appeal to the children. Whenever I have taken animated soft toys or puppets to training courses, the almost magnetic pull these characters have never fails to amaze me. There are sometimes universal favourites but everyone wants to pick up and handle all of them. I think it is a little part of our childhood that thankfully we never lose.

You could begin by browsing around local toyshops or by searching through the many catalogues or websites available for a good quality puppet. There is a huge variety of excellent puppets for you to choose from to suit a range of budgets. If you are not quite ready to invest in a commercially sourced puppet, remember that many soft toys can become animated with the help of some simple handwork and a little imagination. My first puppet, which was a favourite of my nursery children and still helps me to share stories with young children today, actually belonged to one of my own children. It is not very sophisticated but then puppets don't always have to be; each will have a unique appeal and a character that is all its own.

If you are feeling really brave you might like to try making a puppet from scratch using a basic pattern and some simple materials. You could even adapt a soft toy which has had some or all of the stuffing removed from its casing. Remember to carry out some simple safety checks to make sure features such as eyes and nose are secure before introducing it to the children.

Whatever you decide, it is important that your puppet presents itself in the highest quality you can achieve. Apart from the fact that children deserve the very best you can offer them, you must look to the future and the long and happy association you, together with a succession of delighted children, can hope to have with your puppet. A good puppet needs to be built to last and should be maintained in tip-top condition so that it can continue to give pleasure for many years to come.

Setting up a home

Your next responsibility is to find somewhere for your puppet to live. Puppets are very choosy and don't relish the idea of being tossed into a cardboard box or cupboard with other toys after meeting with the children each day! Seriously though, to really help children engage in the learning, you must do everything in your power to sustain the children's belief in the puppet and its world.

You could use a colourful box with a lid or a suitcase or an attractive cloth bag with a gathered top. Consider using a picnic basket or simply have a beautiful piece of fabric, like a silk sarong, which you carefully unfold when it is time for the children to meet the puppet. At this stage, decide how you will take the puppet from its home as well as how you will return it at the end of each session. Perhaps choose to have a special signal, sound, chant or routine that precipitates the arrival of your puppet. Some settings I have visited have a dedicated shelf or seat for their puppet on a display wall. I tend to favour having the puppet out of sight between appearances as this approach helps to maintain an air of mystery and expectation around the puppet and keeps the magic alive.

Creating a puppet profile

What makes each of us unique is the fact that our personalities are made up of a multitude of components that combine to make us who we are. We all live our lives slightly differently to anyone else. With this in mind, you will need to give some careful thought to planning your puppet's character to include elements of its personality and all aspects of its lifestyle. Such planning will enable you to present the puppet over and over again to the children without fear that it will act out of character, doing or saying something that might cause you to lose credibility with your audience.

Children are the keenest of observers and are likely to pick up on any inconsistency. You will need to get your facts right and be confident that you know your puppet better than anyone else. Be prepared to answer knowledgeably any questions that the children might ask. Why not create a passport for your puppet that could be shared with the children when you introduce their new friend to them? This is a good way of giving the children an accurate insight into the puppet's life and it is useful to refer back to from time to time. If you are using more than one puppet, don't forget to include a photograph so that it is easy to match the passport to the correct puppet. Opposite is an example of what it might look like.

Start off by presenting the children with a general outline of your puppet's life. You can then have fun watching your puppet's personality grow and develop as time goes on. All of this experience will help you to create a context within which you and your puppet can relate to the children.

Props and paraphernalia

Now is a good time to be thinking about gathering up resources that will help you and your puppet enter into all kinds of situations for you and the children to explore. Keep your eyes open wherever you are for items that could be used as props for imaginative play or to prompt discussion when you are talking to the children. Props are wonderful for allowing you to set the scene for particular kinds of talk with your children. With a few simple accessories, you can take your puppet forward and back in time and introduce new concepts or experiences to the children. When I use my puppet in this way I think of it as a courier transporting things in and out of the real or imaginary world for the children to explore. When the puppet has brought a present to share with everyone, it generates real excitement and the object becomes much more interesting than if I had simply produced it out of a bag.

Gathering together resources for your prop box can be great fun but be warned; it is seriously addictive and once you start it is difficult to stop! Be reassured that this does not necessarily mean your hobby needs to be an expensive one. Browse around secondhand shops or car boot events and be vigilant during sales. It's amazing what will catch your eye once you start shopping with a puppet in mind.

Imagine the strange looks I got last year when I took my large girl puppet out of a

Puppet Passport

My name is: **Ben**
My Age: **I am 4 years old**

Where I live:	**in the magic story box**
I live with:	**Mum and sister Lily**
My best friends are:	**Mary and Jamilla**
My favourite food is:	**baked beans**
I am happy when I am:	**drawing pictures**
I get sad when:	**nobody plays with me**
I am afraid of:	**spiders and snakes**
My favourite toy is:	**Fuzzy Wuzzy the rabbit**

bag in the clothing department of a supermarket so that she could try on a sparkly party dress in the spring sales. She needed to look the part for her imminent debut as a pop star - complete with a karaoke microphone!

There are lots of basic costume and accessory ideas listed on page 62 of this book but there are endless possibilities, so you can look forward to adding to your prop box over and over again.

Puppet practice - makes perfect

Let's get one thing out of the way for a start - puppets do not come with 'L' plates! You might feel like a novice but no-one else will think of you in that way. You may feel self-conscious about other adults watching you but it may reassure you to know that, in my experience, people who watch other adults using puppets have only one thing on their mind - and that is sheer admiration! You will soon realise that everyone is so transfixed and absorbed in the puppet that the focus is rarely on you and how well you are doing.

You need to gain confidence in handling particular puppets and decide upon the various ways of operating them that work best for you. The more practice you have, the more comfortable you will feel with your new partner. Spend some time sitting in front of a mirror practising a few basic moves and you will no doubt surprise yourself how convincing it all looks. You are likely to be your own worst critic!

Using your puppets effectively

Some people shy away from using puppets because they suffer from what I call the Vaudeville complex; the notion that for puppets to be brought to life successfully there needs to be some kind of all-singing,

all-dancing approach on the part of the handler. This could not be further from the truth. It is often the case that the less sophisticated you are in terms of your technique, the more effective you are in engaging the children with the character and the subtleties of meaning you are trying to convey.

I think puppets can be classified according to the manner in which they are deployed. There are three distinct operational groups, which I affectionately call watchers, warblers or whisperers. You might decide to combine all three techniques but at this stage, it is important to decide which direction you are going to take and with which particular puppets. This will depend largely on the purpose for which you are using them.

Watcher puppets, for example, are ideal if you simply want to introduce a new friend to the children. This works well when you are settling in new children who are learning to be part of a group. This particular puppet could come out just for story times, helping you to handle the book carefully or demonstrating good looking and listening skills. You can praise your puppet friend constantly for paying attention to the story and hopefully this will encourage the children to focus too. Watchers can be really effective but they do rely on you to animate them carefully; it's a good example of actions speaking louder than words. Helping your puppet to react to different situations by simply moving its head in a variety of ways can convey a range of emotions and feelings to the children.

Some practitioners incorporate watcher puppets into displays - helping to define areas of their environments, perhaps to establish particular rules such as being tidy with the toys or to encourage individuals to engage in some form of independent learning. A colleague in an Early Years setting recently told me about her 'Number Gnome' who was in residence in her maths area of the playroom. He was notorious for mixing up the numbers on the hanging number line when no one was looking and the children apparently loved sorting out the materials following each of his mischievous pranks. However, I do have reservations about the deployment of a puppet in a watching capacity as a kind of 'sleeping policeman' who reports back to the practitioner whenever a child has been observed carrying out some misdemeanour. However tempting it might be to use a puppet in this way, I believe that this practice can often break down any crucial trust the children have invested in the puppet. Puppets should be viewed first and foremost as friends who only notice when children are being helpful and kind towards one another.

The whisperer category is by far the most common way in which practitioners use puppets with young children and is possibly the most effective means of making a positive start. These kinds of puppet say something quietly in your ear which you then relay back to the children. It is easy to use a puppet in this way as you can literally go with the flow, allowing the children's reactions and responses to move the scenario or discussion along. It is impossible to stick to any script where young children are concerned and you certainly cannot predict their responses.

One real advantage of working with a whispering puppet is that while the puppet is talking quietly in your ear, you have the chance to think about what you are going to say next. Another supportive factor is the tendency for such puppets to present themselves as being rather shy. As a consequence the children tend to

respond, often with great sensitivity, to their new friend.

Warblers, or puppets to whom you give a voice, are best reserved for the more extrovert or experienced practitioner, although this does not necessarily mean that the ability to work in a successful partnership with a talking character is the epitome of puppet handling. Having said this, there can be no denying the charismatic power of a puppet which speaks and responds to the children directly - and the good news is you don't need to become a ventriloquist to bring your character into the children's arena!

Undoubtedly, you will worry about the fact that the children can see your lips moving as you give your puppet a voice. Be prepared for statements like: "It's not real - it's you that's making it talk!" This tends to happen quite often, understandably enough, in the early stages of introducing a puppet to children but it can be dealt with easily. Invariably, each puppet handler will have their own way of overcoming this teething problem. I have had little difficulty getting over this with simple retorts such as: "Yes, my puppet friend needs me to help him to talk to you. Look, this is how I help him to move as well". You might like to get these concerns out of the way at the very beginning - but how you do it is entirely up to you. After all, you know the children best and you will be aware of the need to adapt the information you offer according to the age and stage of the group you are working with.

I met a wonderful puppeteer at a country show this year who had a fabulous home-made puppet which drew everyone to him like a magnet. While chatting to him, I asked him how he overcomes 'The Emperor's New

Clothes' or P.C.S. (Perceptive Child Syndrome) as I call it!

"Sometimes," he said with a smile, "a child will come up to me and say: 'Your dog's not real!'" He explained to me that his universal reaction was to immediately cover both of the puppet's ears protectively and to speak to the child conspiratorially, saying: "Look, it's like this. You know he's not real and I know he's not real but we all enjoy pretending he is real. So let's carry on with this fun game, shall we?" He told me that this usually does the trick. As I said before, it is a personal issue - between you and your puppet really!

There can be no denying that talking puppets have wonderful pulling power. This extra facility makes the puppet seem more convincing and its character more rounded for the children. As a practitioner, the ability to use your voice as a tool will move you into another dimension altogether in terms of your puppet presentation. A puppet that engages in this kind of dialogue with children affords new and exciting possibilities for learning and teaching. It provides a means by which you can subtly convey to the children the range of emotions the puppet is experiencing, assisting the bonding process between puppet and audience. Just think about the rich world of expressive language that can be introduced to children. A puppet can help you to lift the lid on this particular Pandora's box by not only giving you the opportunity to explore new words and expressions but also by providing an endless variety of contexts within which to do so. Talking puppets present you with their own unique set of challenges but, in my experience, they are worth conquering over time as the benefits are enormous.

You don't necessarily need to speak in a manufactured voice, just vary your tone a little according to the age of your puppet, its gender or even according to its mood. Anyone who has ever read or told stories to young children is already more than qualified to do this convincingly. Each of us may have a different storytelling style - from the extravagant amateur dramatist to the quiet but compelling. It doesn't matter which category you fall in to, you will have the skills you need to transport your characters into the children's world.

Why puppets have the upper hand

Even within the technically sophisticated world of today's educational materials, the role of the puppet remains quite unique. Puppets are not merely visual aids with a principal function of seducing children into learning, nor are they pre-programmed to respond to the click of a computer mouse. What makes these characters so different is that they have the ability to evolve and adapt to meet a multiplicity of learning and teaching requirements. They are not only willing to be involved in the whole process, they are designed to participate in it.

We know that young children learn best by doing - in fact, we all do. Think back to the last time you purchased a new piece of technical equipment for your home. Products like these tend to arrive with a complex list of instructions. I am sure that, like me, you give up on these after a while and try the 'hands on' approach instead.

Good practice in early education dictates giving children every opportunity to access rich and meaningful play experiences for themselves. Effective learning is dependent upon each child being able to practise a wide range of skills, explore new experiences and be truly active in their learning. In the light of this, you can see why at this stage of the learning journey, materials like workbooks and worksheets are generally thought to be an inappropriate and ineffective means of developing a child's understanding of the world around them. Puppets, on the other hand, are not only physically active in the learning process but also interactive in the way in which they respond to children. This makes them a natural choice as you face the crucial challenge of bringing learning alive for your children.

Presenting puppets to children

The first thing you need to think about is how the children are going to meet the puppet. There are several important factors in getting off to a positive start with this - and one of the most critical is the timing. It is generally best to gather young children together for a focused activity whenever they have had a prolonged period of active and independent play.

Have a dedicated place for the children to meet with you, making sure that everyone is comfortable and in a position where they will be able to see both you and the puppet clearly. I think it works best if you think of your puppet as a gift to the children each time you present it to them. Here's how that works. Imagine a birthday present. It comes all wrapped up in beautiful paper so that you can only guess at what is inside. You cannot always open it straight away and 'having to wait' builds up the suspense - developing a sense of wonder and awe.

Children's television programmes employ this same technique to grasp and hold the attention of young audiences. Having something hidden away waiting to be unwrapped generates a wonderful atmosphere of suspense and helps to set the scene for the arrival of something or someone special. Can you remember as a child waiting patiently for your favourite character to pop out of the music box or wondering at which window the scene would appear on your favourite programme? It is interesting that, although the formats change over the years, the formula remains unchanged. That's because it works!

Let's get back to the puppets. To create magic along these lines you need to think about how you are going to 'wrap up' your puppet as it generally works best if it gets the chance to be welcomed into your setting according to a familiar ritual. My particular trademark is a magic story box but other people achieve the same impact using a suitcase or a cloth bag. Some people go to extra lengths by incorporating other techniques into their puppet-welcoming routine. Although I have not tried it myself, I am intrigued by the idea that you could have some special sound-making mechanism out of sight which heralds the arrival of the puppet. You could use a rain stick or something similar. Little memory chips which you find inside musical birthday cards or on the hinges of children's treasure boxes are particularly ideal for creating a 'wow' factor.

From here on, the possibilities are limitless. Remember that your puppet knows no boundaries. He or she may arrive at your setting from anywhere or any place in time and may quite often decide not to travel alone. The children love it when the puppet brings along a friend for them to meet, a special toy or artefact from their travels or even a book to share with them. It is always a good idea to give the children plenty of opportunity to get to know the puppet well before you spring any additional surprises on them. They will need time to become comfortable with the central character before you introduce any others.

It is very important for young children to feel secure in order for their learning experiences to be successful. In time, however, they will welcome new introductions and this will help you to keep the experience fresh and exciting for them.

One thing is certain - you are never likely to run out of ideas and if you do, remember that there are always lots of variations on a particular theme. Sometimes you just need to vary your repertoire ever so slightly to keep the children interested.

Visitors to and from the world of imagination

I cannot stress enough at this point the important role that you play in not only bringing a puppet to life for the children but, more importantly, keeping it alive. It is a great responsibility and one that cannot be taken too lightly. I think the key words here are 'connectivity' and 'consistency'. Make sure you have allowed yourself to become attuned to your puppet and furthermore are prepared to help it act out its part from the beginning to the end of its appearance in front of the children.

I find it really disappointing when I watch practitioners, who have engaged in wonderful role-play situations with children, suddenly forgetting their responsibilities within this magical realm of fantasy and bringing the harsh world of reality crashing down around the children's ears. This generally signals the designated end of a free play session when the products of individual or collaborative imagination are literally swept away. I know we have all done it without thinking from time to time, but let me offer an illustration, which should set those alarm bells ringing in your ears! It is a good example of where a preoccupation with efficiency often leads to the kind of brusque practices that get in the way of children's sensibilities.

It was some time ago when this realisation really dawned upon me. I remember it happened when I was observing a particularly high-quality interaction between a three-year-old and his key worker in a pre-school. It grew from unremarkable beginnings; the child was pushing a naked doll around the room in a plastic buggy when the practitioner moved in for a chat. She asked where the child was going with his baby and there followed a lovely conversation between the two. The adult went on to suggest that the baby might be cold and when the little boy promptly pulled the doll from the buggy by one arm to go off and find a blanket, she offered to look after the baby. She took the opportunity of course to demonstrate gold-standard parenting skills, holding the baby carefully in her arms and mentioning the importance of supporting the baby's head and holding her close so that she would feel safe.

The little boy was absorbing all this with avid interest - and was even inspired to have a go for himself when someone bellowed those fatal words, *"Tidy-up time!"* The whole setting erupted suddenly into a frenzy of activity, during which plastic bricks, which a few minutes earlier had been the foundations for castles, were pulled apart with vigour and pitched into plastic boxes. And yes, as you have probably already guessed, the baby doll, too, was catapulted by its left leg over the screen into the role-play area storage box - by the practitioner now in functional mode. What a strange and perplexing world it must be for young children where adults act out such inconsistencies!

Children are keen observers and are susceptible to the disorientating effect of mixed messages coming from people they trust. I think many of us have learned to think twice before, for example, picking up a toy dog by its ear and tossing it into a box at tidy-up time, when a few minutes before we were actively demonstrating the finer points involved in handling our pets!

If you relate this to the use of puppets, then you need to ensure that you not only handle your puppet appropriately throughout the session, but also give careful consideration to the closure of your puppet presentation. The children must see the puppet in its animated state at the start of each session and, most importantly, be satisfied that their friend is alive as it returns to the home you have created for it.

A demonstration in animation

Having shared ideas about how to successfully introduce puppets to the children, it is now time to consider some practical ways of helping them to relate and respond. The key to success here, as with any other developing relationship, is linked to the quality of communication. Since the puppet genre is first and foremost a communicating medium, you don't have to try too hard to achieve positive outcomes. With the help of a few simple techniques, you will feel like an expert!

Think about the tools you employ in your day-to-day communications with other people. To make yourself understood, convey your feelings and share your reactions, you rely on others to be receptive to key indicators in your facial expression and your body language. While not all puppets offer the same opportunities to recreate human expression, it is interesting to observe the response of a group of children to even a simple sock or finger puppet. I have come to the conclusion that in terms of puppet sophistication, less is often better than more. Children can pick up even the subtlest clues about a puppet's personality or emotional state and are wonderfully perceptive when presented with the gentlest forms of animation.

Some handling tips follow which you can select from according to the kind of puppet you are using.

Head and eye movements

- Small shaking head movements up and down - suppressed or mischievous laughter.
- Small shaking movements side to side - fear and trembling.
- Chin up - defiance, unwillingness to co-operate.
- Chin down - sadness, sulking, shyness.
- Head erect but turned away from you - rejection or anger.
- Head erect looking at you in close proximity to your face - extreme interest in what you are saying, anticipation.
- Puppet facing you but head pulled back - extreme disbelief or shock.
- Rapid head movements back and forth between you and the children - panic or concern, a need to be reassured.
- Head slowly moving down to puppet's chest - sense of defeat, dismay, embarrassment.
- Head slowly moving up - realisation or sign of feeling reassured.
- Head slowly rubbing on your shoulder - signifies tiredness.
- Head erect inclined towards children - confidence, willingness to be friendly and engage.
- Head inclined towards yours but facing front - affection and trust.
- Head thrown back, eyes searching for something on the ceiling - guilt, voluntary withdrawal from activity.
- Head low and facing away from you - feeling dejected.

Hands, paws and claws

Here are some additional tips for those of you who are lucky enough to have a puppet with hands that you can manipulate:

- Slow wave close to body - shy greeting.
- Rapid wave with arm outstretched - confident and friendly.
- Open hand (palm inward) covering face - shock, embarrassment.
- Open hand (palm facing outward) - dismay, sadness.
- Hand on head - fear or anticipation of shocking event.
- Hand on heart - great depth of feeling or a pleasant surprise.
- Hand on tummy - feeling unwell.
- Finger pointing to temple - attempt to recollect.
- Finger on lip - concern.
- Hand down by side, fingers bunched - restraint or determination.

With all of these pointers, you have probably realised the importance of both eye movement and levels of eye contact. It is really good practice for your puppet to look at each child in turn as he or she addresses the group. This not only helps to keep everyone's attention and makes them feel included, it also gives the impression that the puppet is speaking with some authority. You have probably noticed politicians employing the same technique when they are trying to be at their most convincing.

Conversely, the avoidance of any kind of eye contact is also part of the powerful messaging system which interplays between individuals, in this case, indicating the withdrawal of support or approval. Children often enjoy watching your puppet play these kinds of mind games with you!

Fabric friends for the Foundation Stage - linking the learning

Puppets as a link to learning

As soon as you begin to use puppets you will be amazed at how easily they support the development of children's understanding across all areas of the curriculum. You will have great fun thinking up ways to involve them in your work, making learning more vibrant and fun for you and the children. Listed below are some ways in which the successful use of puppets can enable you to make effective links with learning. There are also some useful ideas to help you get started.

Personal, social and emotional development

Puppets are a particularly powerful medium within the crucial area of a child's personal, social and emotional development. 'Behaviour and the development of moral values, like dispositions, are heavily influenced by what children observe from adults who are close to them. Small children learn a great deal through imitation.' (Marion Dowling; Young Children's Personal, Social and Emotional Development, Paul Chapman Publishing.)

Puppets support learning by enabling children to:

- feel increasingly secure and develop a sense of trust in the adults in their setting.

- raise their levels of self-confidence and self-esteem.

- develop a strong sense of self and an increasing awareness of the needs and opinions of others. Adults using puppets need to ensure that they act as role models to help children develop inclusive attitudes towards other individuals or groups. Carefully planned scenarios give children the opportunity to stand in other people's shoes and explore how they might feel.

- learn how to foster and sustain friendships through respectful listening to others, sharing ideas and emotions and taking turns in conversation.

- learn about relationships and what is required of an individual in order to become a successful member of a social group. Working alongside the puppet allows children to enter into a variety of different situations and encourages them to make decisions about how they might behave themselves or act towards their peers.

- learn to embrace and enjoy new experiences which encourages the development of positive attitudes towards learning.

- confront and make sense of their feelings and fears. It is very important for young children to have the chance to act out or discuss such issues within a situation in which they feel safe.

Some ideas to try out for yourselves:

- Read or tell stories in which your character finds itself in a particular dilemma but manages to achieve a positive outcome with a little help from his friends. Sometimes the story might be open-ended. Invite the children to provide a solution. *The Power of Puppets* by Georgia Thorp contains scripts for puppet stories and you can use these as a starting point. Alternatively, have fun inventing your own stories.

- Involve your puppets in role-play scenarios that lend themselves to discussion about particular feelings. This encourages the children to empathise with the character.

- To stimulate discussion, use props such as a broken toy, a lost teddy, a birthday party invitation, a photograph or even a dream catcher.

- Create a time-line of photographs taken indoors and out showing your puppet acting out different aspects of your daily routine. Display the timeline to help the children feel secure and develop a sense of ownership of their setting.

Communication, language and literacy

'Communication, language and literacy depend on learning and being competent in a number of key skills, together with having the confidence, opportunity and encouragement, support and disposition to use them. This area of learning includes communication, speaking and listening in different situations and for different purposes…' (QCA Curriculum Guidance for the Foundation Stage). Puppets are at the peak of their effectiveness when it comes to getting young children's language development off to a positive start. They can help you to provide a stimulating starting point from which rich dialogue can flow. We know that children are more effective communicators when they are really interested and excited in an activity. The fact that the puppets are willing to take on any role you ask of them makes it possible for you to set the learning within a variety of appropriate contexts.

Puppets support this area of learning by:

- providing opportunities for children to talk and interact with others -

recounting or recreating experiences, making observations and sharing ideas. This helps to increase their confidence in speaking out in a group.

- providing opportunities for children to develop an early love of books and stories and enjoy rhymes and songs.

- exploring the meaning and various uses of print in the children's environment.

- offering incentives for children to make marks and write for real purposes in the ways they see adults do.

- modelling appropriate use of language in a variety of contexts.

- helping to develop children's phonetic awareness through active play.

- providing opportunities for children to explore and practise aspects of non-verbal communication. This is especially vital for children with communication difficulties.

Some ideas to try out for yourself:

- Make the most of key events in the puppet's life, such as a birthday or a family event. Incorporate these into your setting. Encourage discussion around these events and involve the children in the preparations and festivities: making cards, compiling lists and writing letters.

- Provide the puppet with interesting items or objects for the children to describe and discuss. The children love it when their friend has something hidden in a box or bag for them to unwrap. Try going on a treasure hunt with your puppet; you or the puppet could provide the clues. The activity will help you to check for understanding among the children.

- Create a diary for your puppet. Ask the children to provide drawings and captions or use photographs for the children to use as prompts to help them recall past events in the puppet's life.

- If you can, employ your puppet as a scribe to help you demonstrate different forms of writing. A white board or low flip chart is ideal for this. If you are lucky enough to have a puppet with working hands then your puppet will have no difficulty in holding a pen satisfactorily. If not, then a mouth or beak will work equally well!

- Encourage the children to write letters to their puppet and wherever possible help them to make simple books in which they can record their puppet's adventures in pictures and through emergent writing.

- Invite your puppet to participate in sound discrimination games to help the children develop an early grasp of phonics. Many practitioners find that using puppets really helps to keep the learning interactive and fun - especially when the character gets mixed up with the sounds. The children enjoy not only spotting the mistakes but also being able to help their friend succeed the next time.

Mathematical development

The QCA Guidance for the Foundation Stage suggests that, among other key considerations to promote effective learning in this area, children must be able to access activities that are imaginative and enjoyable. Too many practitioners are limited in their view of what mathematical learning should look like in Early Years settings. Consequently, much of this work with young children centres on adult-constructed table-top activities with materials which rarely motivate children and often fail to sustain their interest.

Puppets are extremely liberating when it comes to this aspect of learning as they free you from other constraints and children can engage in learning which is meaningful, imaginative and enjoyable.

Puppets support this area of learning by:

- helping children to enjoy mathematical learning because they see it being used in real-life situations.

- developing children's confidence in their own ability to think mathematically.

- helping to generate an enthusiasm for learning and encouraging children to participate in practical problem-solving tasks during play.

- providing contexts which promote rich mathematical dialogue between the puppet and the children.

Activities to try out for yourself:

- Present the puppet with simple problems to solve and invite the children to help out. Perhaps a box of small toys has been accidentally spilled and needs sorting. Vary the nature of the challenge according to the learning you are trying to achieve.

- The puppet brings along a bead necklace he has made for a friend. He has forgotten to tie a knot in one end. He can remember the pattern but needs help to repeat it.

- The puppet unravels a number line with pegs for the children to admire but when you help him to display it, something is not quite right. Can the children identify where the puppet has gone wrong and put it right on the line?

- The puppet has brought along a bag of sweets to share with his friends. Have some other puppets or soft toys sitting around. Challenge the children to help the puppet to share fairly.

- Similarly, invite your puppet to have a snack with the children. Put out the wrong number of plates or cups, too few or too many. Involve the children in some practical addition and subtraction. Children love mistakes, particularly when an adult gets it wrong!

- Play pitching games with beanbags and buckets. Pretend the puppet and the children are visiting the seaside or a fairground. Encourage them to use a simple tally to keep the score.

Knowledge and understanding of the world

The Early Learning Goals for Knowledge and Understanding of the World form the basis of future work in science, design and technology, history, geography and information technology - quite a tall order for even the most experienced practitioner! The good news is that puppets can be used to help meet many of the learning and teaching challenges presented in this area of development.

Puppets are naturally curious and are often brave explorers. This 'Indiana Jones' aspect of their personalities makes them a natural choice when it comes to leading the children into the world of new experiences. They help children to:

- develop investigative skills by demonstrating a multi-sensory approach to new experiences which promote understanding.

- develop effective observational skills by drawing children's attention to key features of their environment.

- recognise differences and similarities in features of the natural world and be aware of signs which indicate change.

- realise the importance of key events in their lives and develop an interest in other people's lives.

- develop their natural curiosity by being a willing and active partner in their discoveries. Puppets can offer up emotional responses to new experiences such as surprise and excitement which help promote children's disposition to learn.

- be confident to ask questions, contribute to discussion and offer opinions.

- make connections between past and present experiences.

- make sense of aspects of their own culture and beliefs and explore elements of other cultures. Puppets help tremendously here by role-modelling positive and accepting attitudes towards other people.

Some ideas to try out for yourself:

- Transform your puppet into a pirate complete with eye-patch and hat. He could bring along a treasure chest containing mementoes from his travels, providing your puppet with exciting opportunities to bring interesting objects into your setting for the children to explore together. It could be something from another part of the world or your locality. Encourage the children to smell, touch and perhaps listen to the object to see if it makes a special sound.

- Use props such as spectacles, a white coat and a bow tie to turn your puppet into a professor or dress it up as a detective, complete with magnifying glass. The puppet can demonstrate good 'looking skills' and draw children's attention to key features of special objects brought in from outside.

- Give your puppet magic powers, to enable it to take the children forward or back in time. Turn a special container into a time capsule in which you can hide away photographs of past events in the children's lives or in the corporate life of your setting. The time capsule will also provide you with a hiding place for interesting objects from other times.

- Introduce your puppet's friends to the children, making sure that you include characters from other cultures. This will help the children to gain an insight into the lives of other people. If you are not fortunate to have puppets that reflect other cultures, then use carefully selected multicultural books and let the puppet share stories about the central character with the children. Invent some imaginary penfriends for the children to send letters to. They will look forward to receiving the replies and finding out about their faraway friends. You could even ask your puppet to act as the postman.

- Take your puppets on a photo shoot and capture them in a variety of different settings locally or further afield. You may already have a travelling teddy who goes on adventures with willing grown-ups and comes back with lots of photographs to show the children. The next section of the book shows you how you can get the most out of photographs using puppets.

Physical development

Here are some of the ways puppets can help you to work towards the Early Learning Goals for health and bodily awareness:

- Involve the children in helping puppets to make healthy choices. They will enjoy offering advice. Give the puppet a shopping bag and decide with the children which foods can be eaten in large amounts and which are best reserved as treats. Be careful to avoid judgmental terminology such as 'good' food and 'bad' food.

- Dress your puppet as a doctor or nurse and have some props such as a stethoscope to initiate a discussion about how our bodies work. Your puppet could even lead a keep-fit session, prompting some useful discussion about the changes that take place in our body when we are active.

- Try waking your puppet up at the start of an activity session and encouraging it to go back to sleep after having fun with the children. I usually remark on how tired my puppet is looking as the session comes to an end. It is a good time to remind everyone of the need for our bodies to rest after we have worked it hard.

Creative development

Because puppets have an endless repertoire of interesting scenarios to share, they are a wonderful trigger for firing up children's imagination. The Early Learning Goal for this area of Creative Development states that by the end of the Foundation Stage most children will be able to: 'Use their imagination in art and design, music, dance, imaginative role play and stories' (QCA Curriculum Guidance for the Foundation Stage).

It would be difficult to highlight specific activities likely to promote creative learning in relation to the use of puppets. This is because puppets simply can't help making the learning happen; they lead children into the magical world of imagination every time they meet!

Puppets are such natural partners for stories and role-play that once you start using them, you might well find yourself wondering why you haven't invited them before.

It is really important that children have lots of opportunities to handle puppets independently and to use them to help recreate real life as well as to develop imaginary scenarios in their play. It is equally important, however, that you provide the children with an additional set of puppets to those that you routinely use in front of them. If the children's belief is to be sustained, it is vital that your puppets are not mishandled or allowed to act out of character.

This section contains photographs, photocopiables and resource lists with practical notes to stimulate and support your work

Putting puppets in the frame - using photographs to support learning

Going on a puppet photo shoot

I am a real fan of large puppets such as those illustrated in this book. They are an ideal size for handling and are essentially child-like which makes them popular with children. I have chosen four large puppet friends to appear in the pictures and I hope they will introduce you to the wealth of learning and teaching possibilities that arise when you use photographs like these.

Imagine the scene. It is early morning and I step out of my front door armed with several puppets, two rolling pins, sticky tape and a digital camera. These are the tools of an intrepid puppet photographer ready for a morning's work. Be warned, unless your neighbours know you well, you are going to invite a great deal of curtain twitching! Ask anyone who has got into the unique craft of puppet photography and they will tell you that what starts off as a bit of a lark turns into a real obsession. The amazing thing about puppets is that they are so photogenic. Put them into a real-life situation, take their photograph and prepare to be amazed at how life-like they have become.

You will need to employ some simple techniques to help you to present your puppets in the most convincing way - which brings me to the painful subject of the rolling pins. I find them invaluable in helping my puppets adopt any standing pose but I want to reassure you that no puppets were harmed in the making of this book! Sticky parcel tape is another useful thing to have in your toolkit, ideal for putting hands into different positions or for helping friends to hold on to each other. Where something stronger is called for, try pins with large plastic heads, such as those used on notice boards. These are great for attaching puppet clothing to objects in the immediate background and help you to create more subtle poses.

Home and away

You don't need to venture too far afield to get some great pictures. Not everyone is comfortable with the idea of heading out to take puppet photographs in the full gaze of curious strangers. As a result of this, the photographs featured in this book were taken in and around my own home and garden. There is always plenty of scope for developing the children's learning no matter what your starting point.

Having photographs of the puppets in a home situation to share with the children can really work to your advantage. The children will enjoy gathering information about where the puppets live and will be interested to find out what their house looks like, what kind of toys they play with and other details surrounding their life out of your setting.

It is really advantageous if you can use the bedroom of your own child or one belonging to the child of a willing friend in which to take photographs of your puppets. In this privileged position, you will enjoy access to unlimited child-friendly props to help you to set up and capture all sorts of play-based situations in pictures. Having photographs of your puppets in a child's setting really helps to capture children's imagination, enabling them to see the puppets as fellow members of their own very special kind.

For the more adventurous, head out to a nearby park, a local shop, fast-food place or into the countryside and take photographs of the puppets in situations with which the children are familiar. You will be surprised at how co-operative people will be when you invite them to be involved in your picture-making session. I have seen wonderful photographs of puppets visiting the doctor, talking to a friendly policeman or even having their hair cut at the local hairdresser's. Most people will relish having the chance to be a celebrity for the day!

Here is a useful tip for those of you still feeling nervous about going out and about with your puppets - take some children along to help you. This gives you a perfect excuse to do something a little off-beat. Pack up your puppets together with a sense of adventure and anticipate the wonderful response you will generate.

It is not always possible to take children out of the setting to experience things at first-hand but puppet photographs present a really effective alternative. They offer an interesting and exciting way to help children learn about the world around them.

Using themes to inspire learning

While I don't want to spoil anyone's fun by suggesting the need to plan your photographs in detail before you start,

I think it really helps to have an idea about the kinds of learning and the discussion and ideas you hope the photographs will prompt. Begin by having some basic themes in the back of your mind. This will enable you to build up a useful photo library over time. You will be able to dip in and out of this resource to support future learning within your planned programme or to help you explore issues that arise spontaneously.

Here are some suggested categories into which your photographs might fall:

- Exploring feelings
- Likes and dislikes
- Making friends
- Happy times
- Fears and tears
- Making choices
- Out and about

Helping the children to interpret a variety of different social contexts will have a significant bearing on both their developing social skills as well as their ability to communicate. This allows you to push the boundaries of their experience. The photographs are a stimulus for dialogue and they provide a forum for children to have their voices heard and to listen to one another. It's as simple as that.

How to use the support materials in this book

Using the photographs

The photographs that appear in this section can be used in a variety of ways. In the first instance, I hope you have as much fun looking at them as I had taking them and that they encourage you to have a go for yourself. The large format pictures are ideal for sharing with small groups of children as a stimulus for discussion. Each one presents you with a particular theme to explore and develop.

Even if you don't have access to large puppets, the photographs make it possible for you to successfully introduce the characters to your children and bring them to life in their imaginations. You can even turn them into soap-opera stars by bringing out the book from time to time and using each photograph in turn to help you to create a new episode together.

You may find it particularly useful to select photographs to deal with specific issues that develop among your children, for example, when you notice a child is being excluded during play. Conversely, you can use individual images to help you to positively reinforce appropriate social behaviour by asking questions like: "Can you see in the picture that the friends are helping each other - just like Zoe and Ralph were doing at tidy-up time?"

For ease of reference and to give you an idea about possible themes, this section of the book provides you with a range of photographs and an accompanying set of brief practitioner's notes. The notes are not intended to be in any way prescriptive; they are just a few ideas to help you get started.

You will have plenty of ideas of your own and so will the children - they are masters of interpretation. Prepare yourself for very intuitive and entertaining responses!

Using the cartoon sheets

This section also contains a set of black and white line drawings which correspond to each photograph. The pages are suitable for photocopying or enlarging and can be used either with small groups or with individual children.

These sheets provide an ideal follow-up to discussions about the photographs, providing you with a starting point for stories or a means for recording the children's ideas about what the puppet characters might be saying or thinking. You could act as a scribe, recording the words of the children in the thought clouds or speech bubbles. Alternatively, make it possible for the children to access the sheets during independent play. This is often when the most successful emergent writing takes place.

Always ensure that the children have the opportunity to select from a wide range of resources likely to stimulate this early mark-making and encourage emergent writing. For example, the photographs of the new baby or the puppet girl who is ill in bed might prompt some children to write letters or make cards. It is so important that young children are able to freely access the resources they need to allow these vital learning experiences to happen.

Tricks of the trade

I hope this 'behind the scenes' glimpse of

the magical world of puppets captures your imagination and helps to broaden the horizons of your puppet landscape. By providing you with some understanding of the basic tricks of the trade, it should offer up some possible starting points for developing your own work with these characters. At the end of this section, you will find a collection of suggested props and accessories designed to enhance your puppet's appearances in front of the children. I am sure you will find yourself adding to this list again and again as your enthusiasm grows. In view of this, I have also left space for you to record your own notes and ideas.

And finally...

I was lucky enough to spend a week going out and about in Cornwall visiting Early Years settings with my storytelling puppet recently. A respected colleague who is an Early Years tutor at a local college contacted me beforehand to ask if she could sit in on one of my sessions in a school reception class. At the end, I went across to greet her and enjoyed the usual warm response. She smiled at me and said, with what I understood to be real sincerity, "Linda, can I say that I consider it a real privilege to watch you work with young children…"

I was thinking that this must surely be one of the high points in my career, until she added, "You see, you are so completely off your trolley!"

Well, I decided in the end that this was indeed a compliment. After all, if you cannot make learning fun and exciting for children of this age, then you must ask yourself where you are going wrong.

Enjoy working with puppets. Make friends with these wonderful characters and you will reap the many benefits of this loyal and supportive partnership in learning and teaching for many years to come. The adventure, as they say, is only beginning…

Story time

Puppets are excellent for helping you to deliver a successful story-time session. Using the puppet to help you introduce a book to the children and demonstrate good listening skills really affords you many opportunities to make the most of this special time together. Try having a special puppet who lives in a magic story box. The children will be eager to come together as a group and await the arrival of their friend!

Suggested themes for extension work:
- Making friends
- Happy times/sad times
- Exploring feelings
- Likes and dislikes

Helpful questions to ask the children:
- What can you see happening in the picture?
- Why do you think the friends are smiling?
- What is your favourite book?
- What do you think is happening in the story they are reading?

Follow-up ideas:
- Group story writing: make a book for the puppets to share. You could provide a starting point for a story and the children could suggest what happened next. You can record the story on a white board or on a flip chart so that the children can see their story take shape. It is really important that children have the opportunity to see adults demonstrate writing for different purposes. When the book is complete, the children can illustrate parts of it with their drawings. How about putting the children's finished book in the magic story box as a present to the puppet while he is asleep? The next time the puppet visits, he will be eager to thank them and enjoy reading their story back to them.
- Encourage children to paint pictures of their favourite stories or parts of a story. You can tell the story behind each child's painting by scribing underneath what the child says about the picture.

Don't sit under the apple tree...

This photograph offers many opportunities for you to explore a challenging aspect of a child's personal, social and emotional development. Within any social grouping, there are times when everyone experiences moments of exclusion or isolation. Young children need you to help them make sense of these feelings and this photograph offers a useful starting point for discussion. Focus with the children on what the puppets might do to make their friend feel included and be able to share in their happy moment.

Suggested themes:
* Making friends
* Happy times/sad times
* Exploring feelings

Helpful questions to ask the children:
* How do you think Jamilla is feeling?
* Why do you think Ben has given Mary a present?
* What kind of presents do you like to get?
* What do you think Ben and Mary could do to help Jamilla feel happy?
* Who is your special friend?

Follow-up ideas:
* Offer children a range of scrap materials which they can select from independently so that they can make a present for Jamilla to help her to feel happy again. They might choose to make a model or draw or paint a picture instead.
* Have a birthday party for your puppet or for Mary, one of the puppets in the picture. Involve children in the preparations - making decorations, special food, party hats and writing invitations or making birthday cards.
* At circle time, with your puppet on your lap, offer the children the prompt: "I feel happy when…"
* Have a variety of wrapped up boxes for the children to pass around. The puppet can help them guess what might be inside.

Snack time

Food is a subject dear to most people's hearts! Children especially love to talk about their favourite treats and are very clear about their particular likes and dislikes. This makes food an ideal topic for discussion. Here, the puppet friends are at the table deciding on a piece of fruit for snack. This helps you to explore the theme of healthy choices linked to food and as there is only one orange, the added dilemma of how the fruit might be shared makes potential discussion even more interesting!

Suggested themes:
- Making friends
- Making choices
- Likes and dislikes

Helpful questions to ask the children:
- What do you think Ben is saying to Mary?
- What fruit do you think each friend is going to choose for their snack?
- Which piece of fruit would you choose?
- What should they do if they both want to have the orange?

Follow-up ideas:
- Help your children to make a fruit salad for a snack. Invite your puppet to join you. The children can set the table and share the food out so that everyone has an equal share.
- Help children to make a chart of foods which are really healthy to eat and those which it is better to save for occasional treats. Remember to be non-judgmental and accepting of all children's suggestions.
- Present your puppet to the children with a stomach ache! Help the children to find out what the puppet ate that made him feel so unwell. The children will enjoy giving him advice about sensible eating for the future!
- At circle time, offer the prompt: "My favourite fruit is..." or " I like to eat..."

Not speaking

Even in the wonderful world of puppets, friendships have their moments of doubt! Here is an ideal springboard for talk about what makes us angry or upset. Resolving conflict is a tricky problem for grown-ups, even though they have a great deal of experience to fall back on in times of trouble. Entering into the world of the puppet friends will help you to explore such issues in a non-threatening way, giving children permission to express their own frustrations and anxieties as they build friendships of their own.

Suggested themes:
- Making friends
- Happy times/sad times
- Exploring feelings

Helpful questions to ask the children:
- What do you think is happening in the picture?
- Why do you think the friends are not looking at each other?
- How do you think they are feeling?
- What do you think will happen next?

Follow-up ideas:
- Look for age-appropriate storybooks with themes of friendship. These often have a hint of problems that can arise even between the best of friends. Thankfully, the storylines usually offer solutions that lead to happy endings! Have a puppet friend on-hand to share the story time with the children.
- Present your puppet to the children in a disgruntled mood, perhaps adopting the arms crossed, lack of eye contact pose portrayed in the photograph. Encourage the puppet to relay to the children what happened between the puppet and his friend. Invite the children to suggest how the two puppets might become friends again.
- Your puppet can bring along a special soft toy friend which he passes around the group. The children are invited to tell the toy: "My friend is …". Be vigilant for children who are not named and be ready to include them when it is your turn or that of the puppet.

Meet the baby

A key event in the life of many young children is the arrival of a new baby in their world. Some children deal with the advent of a baby brother or sister in an altogether positive way while others find the situation confusing and unsettling. The puppets in the photograph look on, while the baby in the picture features centre stage. This photograph is sure to encourage a great deal of talk among your children and this will enable you to recognise and allay any anxieties that the children might have.

Suggested themes:
- Exploring feelings
- Making friends
- Caring for others

Helpful questions to ask the children:
- What do you think the friends are saying to each other?
- How can they look after the baby?
- Who do you think the baby belongs to?

Follow-up ideas:
- Your puppet can bring a box or bag of interesting bits and pieces belonging to a baby. The children can pass the bag around and take things from it to talk about and share.
- Let the puppet visit with a 'puppet baby'. Encourage the children to bring along photographs to show their puppet friends - either of themselves as babies or of a baby brother or sister.
- Invite a mum and her new baby to visit. She can answer questions the children might ask - you can ask some on their behalf where you think there are gaps in their knowledge.
- Provide children with a life-like doll and a few well-chosen baby resources to encourage positive attitudes in your role-play area too. Adults can be on-hand to offer advice and demonstrate the essential caring skills.

Hide and seek

It looks as if an exciting game of hide and seek has taken an unexpected turn for the little girl in the picture. Ben is clearly enjoying playing a trick on his puppet friend. She has searched but cannot find Ben anywhere. She is left feeling a little lonely and scared. This photograph might help you to talk about simple game rules. Establish with the children some basic tips to ensure that everyone plays fairly and happily together - and most importantly that no one gets hurt. Your children will love taking the moral high ground on this one!

Suggested themes:
- Making friends
- Happy times/sad times
- Exploring feelings

Helpful questions to ask the children:
- What do you think is happening in the picture?
- How do you think Mary is feeling?
- What games do you like to play with your friends outside?
- What do you think will happen next?

Follow-up ideas:
- Play games on the theme of hide and seek. Perhaps your puppet is sad because he has lost a favourite toy somewhere in the garden or outdoor play area. The children could listen to the description and then go off to find it for him.
- Hide a large amount of small toys such as plastic animals in and around your setting - preferably in a secure outdoor play area. Provide the children with small paper bags and invite them to gather up as many as they can. When they return to the group, encourage them to describe to others where they found their toys.
- Another good idea is to have your puppet lead a paper trail with clues for the children to find some 'treasure'. They will need to listen very carefully to the clues!

Secrets can seem very exciting to children but there is a need for ground rules if no one is to be left feeling excluded or hurt. We can see Ben is whispering something in Mary's ear and they both look happy to be sharing this particular secret. Perhaps they are planning a lovely surprise for someone special. We can guess together what that secret might be!

Suggested themes:

- Making friends
- Making choices
- Exploring feelings

Helpful questions to ask the children:

- What do you think Ben is saying to Mary?
- Do you think it is a secret? How do you know?
- What do you think the secret is about?

Follow-up ideas:

- Talk with the children about the picture, using the question prompts above. Use these as a gentle starting point for a more general talk about 'good secrets' and 'bad secrets' and why it is important to share things with grown-ups whenever we know a secret which makes us feel unhappy or worried.
- Let your puppet bring along some secrets or surprises in a bag or a box. The children will be intrigued to find out what the puppet has brought for them to look at and talk about.
- Use your puppet to help your children develop early phonic awareness in active and fun ways. One game you might try is having the puppet whisper a particular letter sound in your ear. Tell everyone what it is and they can take turns saying the sound softly back in the puppet's ear
- Play 'Chinese Whispers' and pass around everyone's name in turn.

Return to Eden

This one is not for the nervous! Mary is terrified to find a huge snake in the garden when she is outside playing with Ben. She is really afraid of snakes and doesn't even like to see pictures of them in books. Ben is feeling very brave because he knew at once that it was just a soft toy and he helps to reassure her. It is so important to understand children's fears so that you can help to rationalise them. Having this knowledge enables you to take active steps to reassure your children whenever a difficult situation arises. Children need adults to help them develop a similar awareness of, and sensitivity to, other children's anxieties as well.

Suggested themes:
- Fears and tears
- Happy times/sad times
- Exploring feelings

Helpful questions to ask the children:
- What do you think is happening in the picture?
- How do you think Mary is feeling?
- What makes you feel afraid?
- How do you think Ben can help Mary to feel better?
- What might he be saying to her?

Follow-up ideas:
- Wake up your puppet and invite him to join in with your talk. He is still feeling sleepy but tells you that he has had a nightmare. Talk about how it feels to be afraid and quickly follow up with ideas for making everyone feel better again! Be ready - when you have asked for these suggestions, your children will no doubt be eager to give Ben a reassuring cuddle.

- The children's book *We're Going On a Bear Hunt* by Michael Rosen is a great favourite among children and adults alike! The chorus 'We're not scared' helps children to feel powerful when faced with difficult situations.

- Make a list of 'feelings' words for Mary when she saw the snake. Be ready to accept and record the children's original made-up words too!

Everyone loves to receive an invitation - even if it is as simple as being asked out to play as is happening in this picture. It is clearly time for an adventure and only the puppets know where they will be going and where this will lead. Bring that sense of adventure to your setting by using this photograph as a starting point for a shared outing or to announce a planned visit to the setting by someone interesting, such as the local lollipop lady or policeman.

Suggested themes:
* Making friends
* Happy times/sad times
* Out and about

Helpful questions to ask the children:
* What can you see happening in the picture?
* What do you think Ben is saying to his friend?
* Who is your best friend? Where do you like to go together?
* Where do you think these friends are going?

Follow-up ideas:
* Here's a great way to get some rich dialogue going between your puppet and the children! All you need is one chatty puppet, a small group of eager children and two second-hand mobile phone handsets or old telephones. The puppet can telephone the children and ask if he can accompany them for a special day out. Your children will love being able to choose the destination - and they even get to bring a grown-up of their choice along too.
* Offer the children a selection of folded cards, envelopes and blank postcards together with some pens and stickers. They will have great fun making their own cards and 'writing' for real purposes in the ways they see adults do. Have a post-box nearby so they can 'send' their cards too.
* Take your puppets and the children out for an adventure to a nearby park or place of local interest. Take lots of photographs to share with the children back in the setting.

Bedside manners

As you can see from the picture, even puppets can get sick from time to time. Mary is in bed with a bad cold and Ben has come to visit her. This scenario can give rise to much discussion about how it feels to be unwell and what other people can do to help us get better. Children are natural carers and are often quite instinctive about the needs of other people; they just need the chance to test their skills in practical applications.

Suggested themes:
- Making friends
- Happy times/sad times
- Exploring feelings
- Fears and tears

Helpful questions to ask the children:
- What do you think is happening in the picture?
- How do you think Mary is feeling?
- What do you think Ben is saying to her?
- Can you remember a time when you felt unwell?
- What happened to make you better again?

Follow-up ideas:
- Invite children to make a 'Get well' card for Mary.
- Present your puppet tucked up in a doll's cot and encourage the children to ask questions to find out what is the matter. Help the children to take its temperature, pulse and heartbeat, remembering to demonstrate the behaviour and vocabulary appropriate to the situation.
- Ask a local nurse or health visitor to examine your puppet and talk about how we can keep healthy.
- Provide the children with soft toys, beds, blankets and a simple first aid kit so that they can practise their caring skills through role-play.

Practice makes perfect

Ben rather fancies himself as a budding pianist and is quite oblivious to his less than appreciative audience! Children enjoy music and you might use this photograph as a starting point for some sound-making activities of your own. Songs and other musical activities - apart from being a popular inclusion in any daily programme - are a wonderful way of helping children to develop an awareness of rhyme and rhythm. They also provide natural opportunities for children to discriminate between different sounds and thereby develop a child's phonetic awareness.

Suggested themes:
- Exploring feelings
- Making friends
- Likes and dislikes

Helpful questions to ask the children:
- What do you think is happening in the picture?
- Do you think Mary is enjoying Ben's music?
- What do you think she should do?

Follow-up ideas:
- Set time aside each session for you and the children to enjoy a musical activity together. This might be action songs or rhymes, clapping games or enjoying listening to different kinds of music. Encourage children to think about how the various pieces make them feel.

- Have your puppet compere a talent show and invite individuals to take to the stage. Offer plenty of support and give generous helpings of praise. This will help your young children learn the importance of valuing the efforts of others in a group. A toy microphone, especially one which attempts to amplify sound, is a great prop here. Ben could use it to introduce each turn and the child could then hold it. Watch out - soon everyone will want to audition!

- Use a rain stick to help children tune in and listen during sound work. It has a remarkably calming effect. Why not make your own instruments too?

Finding in-roads to established groups is not easy for anyone - let alone a socially inexperienced three- to four-year-old. Here we see a forlorn Ben sitting on the sidelines of what appears to be a very exciting play situation. We don't know whether Ben chose not to play with the group for some reason or if the others upset him or pushed him aside. One thing is for sure, your children will have their own ideas about this emotive photograph. Once you have set the scene with them, they will have plenty of useful advice to offer the characters so that the sad situation might be resolved. After all, everyone loves a happy ending!

Suggested themes:

- Making friends
- Happy times/sad times
- Exploring feelings
- Fears and tears

Helpful questions to ask the children:

- Why do you think Ben is not playing with his friends?
- How do you think he is feeling?
- What could the others do to make him feel better?
- What do you think will happen next?

Follow-up ideas:

- Talk about the activities that individual children enjoy playing most of all.
- Ben has a favourite teddy which he cuddles when he is upset. Talk about the children's comfort toys or objects and value each child's contribution.
- Invite Ben's teddy to be a special visitor for one day. He could tell the children his version of events on the day of the photograph. Focus on how the situation moved on from Ben feeling excluded to being part of the group again.
  The children will find it difficult to interview the teddy so you will have to lead here. You can encourage them to think of solutions where everyone has a fair deal and is treated with kindness.

There is a magical connection between children and animals. Those children who own pets are always happy to talk to others about them. Those who do not are happy to assume joint ownership of someone else's pet, eg "My granny's neighbour has a big dalmation". It is often a good ice-breaker when getting to know children for the first time. And so it was that we established a practice in our nursery, during pre-admission interviews, of asking parents if there were any pets in the family. It was so wonderful to watch a child take those first trusting emotional steps towards you when you were able to name and talk knowledgeably about their cat, dog, rabbit or even goldfish! Here, you can tap into the fascination that children have for these creatures by using this photograph as a springboard for lots of useful discussion.

Suggested themes:

- Making friends
- Exploring feelings
- Fears and tears
- Caring for others

Helpful questions to ask the children:

- What can you see in the picture?
- Do you think Mary likes the tortoise? How do we know?
- What do you think Ben is saying to Mary?
- What do you think will happen next?

Follow-up ideas:

- Read stories to the children, with the help of your storytelling puppet, which centre around caring for small animals.
- Invite some pet owners to visit your setting and talk to the children about how they care for their particular animal.
- Let your puppet bring along a soft-toy pet in a makeshift pet-carrier. Use the pretend telephones to let the children act as the vet, advising your puppet on how to look after their new pet.

Time for a rest?

We all know how much children enjoy being outdoors - especially when there is a hint of adventure attached to their play! Perhaps Ben and Mary have been climbing up and along the walls and Mary feels she wants a rest in the sun, having become exhausted as a result all their energetic play. Ben, on the other hand, is still raring to go and wants to climb even higher! Here is a good chance to talk to the children about how our bodies respond to exercise and for you to do some awareness raising about the benefits of keeping fit and active. Puppets are great for setting good examples!

Suggested themes:

- Making friends
- Exploring feelings
- Health and bodily awareness
- Out and about
- Being safe

Helpful questions to ask the children:

- Can you guess what game Ben and Mary have been playing outside?
- What do you think is happening in the picture?
- What do you think Mary is saying?
- What do you think Ben is saying?
- What do you think happened before this picture?

Follow-up ideas:

- Use a special puppet or soft toy which joins the group each session for some kind of physical activity. I found that my chimpanzee character was a great advocate for fresh air and exercise because he always wanted to be on the go. He is a great motivator for reluctant friends!
- Dress one of your character puppets in sweat-bands with a range of props such as a water bottle and towel to get some talk going about the immediate and longer term effects of exercise on our bodies.

Look to the skies!

Developing effective listening skills and being able to discriminate between one sound and another is crucial to a young child's language skills. Similarly, young children need to be trained if they are to become keen observers. All you need, however, is one interested puppet 'explorer' or 'detective' and something really interesting for everyone to look at and talk about. Whatever route you are following on a child's learning journey, the good news is there are lots of ways to make the adventure exciting for your children. That is, of course, if you remember to take your puppet friends along too!

Suggested themes:

- Out and about
- Making friends
- Fears and tears

Helpful questions to ask the children:

- What do you think happened just before this photograph was taken?
- What do you think the friends are looking at?
- What do you think Ben is saying?
- What do you think Mary is thinking?

Follow-up ideas:

- Play listening games with the children and a blind-folded puppet. The children could say 'good morning' to the puppet in a silly voice and their puppet friend can guess who it was that spoke to him. This is a great activity for helping everyone feel affirmed and recognised as part of the group.
- Have a circle time 'hush' where children listen for sounds around them - "I can hear a..." The old favourite, 'Kim's game' is great for looking skills!

Oops!

Now for a touch of real puppet melodrama! What do you do when you are playing at your friend's house and you accidentally break something very special? You will have no trouble getting your equally boisterous three- to five-year-olds to identify with this scenario. And even perhaps confess to similar crimes! The children will love playing detectives with this one as they try to work out who actually dropped the plate as they begin to interpret the photograph for themselves. The challenge here is to steer the children's talk in such a way as to avoid any kind of blame culture developing. Instead, help the children to focus on how upset the puppet will be and remind them that this can happen to anyone. It is never the end of the world!

Suggested themes:
- Happy times/sad times
- Exploring feelings
- Fears and tears

Helpful questions to ask the children:
- What do you think is happening in the picture?
- Who do you think broke the plate? What makes you think that?
- What do you think Ben is thinking?
- Can you guess what might happen next?
- Have you ever broken something? How did it make you feel?

Follow-up ideas:
- Introduce your puppet to the children when he is feeling very sad one day. Bring along a carrier bag with a broken toy inside to show the group. Fortunately, the children are able to put it back together and soon their friend is happy again. Activities like these send out really positive messages about caring for and understanding the needs of others. Children learn that they are powerful and can make a difference.
- Have a collection of fragile or precious things and teach the children to handle them carefully. They will enjoy having your trust in their ability.

Props and accessories

Resources to support learning

- microphone
- spectacles
- sunglasses
- joke shop items
- home-made telescope
- spyglass
- magnifying glass
- mobile telephone
- binoculars
- special occasion cards
- puppet's own photo album
- puppet's diary
- masks/blindfold
- magician and fairy wands
- pretend food
- old camera
- sparkly treasure chest box
- musical jewellery box
- torch
- bandages
- small toys belonging to the puppet
- comforter/baby blanket
- puppet's suitcase (packed lunch boxes are ideal)
- clear plastic bottle to hide messages in
- hand mirror (look out for novelty ones which have special effects such as lights or sounds)
- sound-making character toys and sound effects from hinges of 'noisy' greetings cards

Costume collection

- child's party dress
- waistcoat/bow-tie
- assorted hats
- dressing-up clothes: fire-fighter's hat, nurse's hat, space-suit, fairy, animals
- neck-scarves
- play tabards
- trainers/boots
- sleepwear
- royal cloak/magician's cape
- character head-gear: crown, tiara, pirate, fire-fighter, nurse
- shopping basket
- back-pack
- handbags
- beads
- medallions
- clip-on earrings

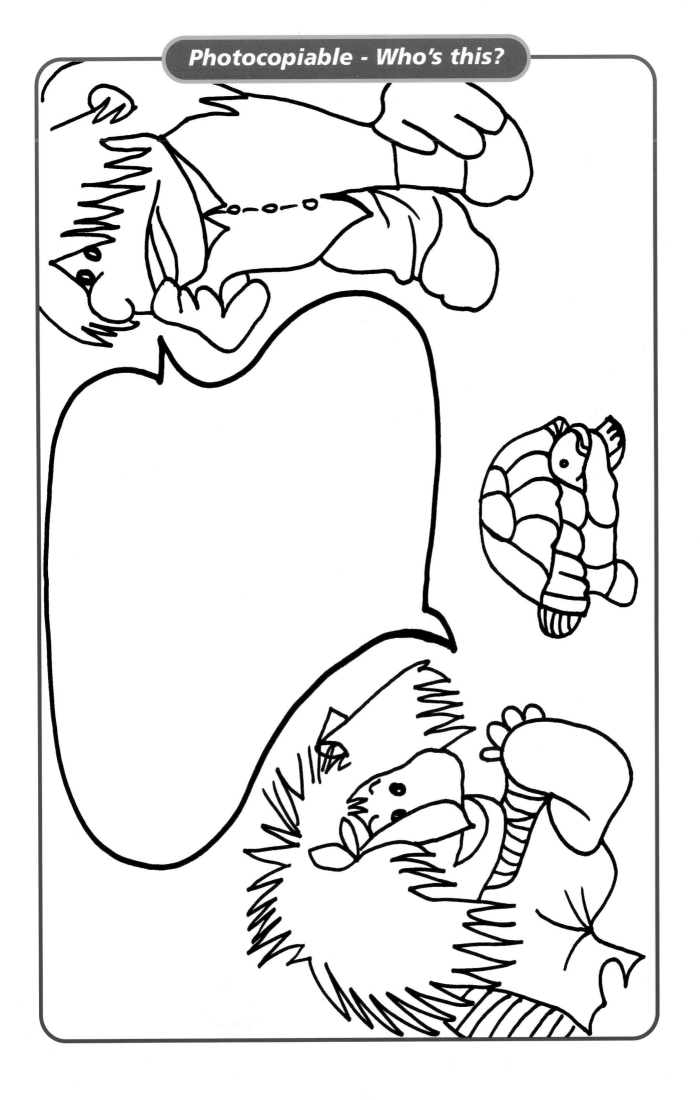

Other books in the series...

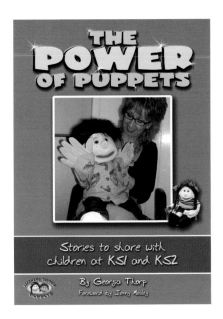

The Power of Puppets

Stories to share with children at KS1 and KS2 by Georgia Thorp

Training For Everyone from Jenny Mosley Consultancies

The Art of Storytelling

Gain insights into how storytelling and story making can contribute to the linguistic, emotional, physical and cognitive development of children.

Puppets at Large

Encourage everyone to get their puppets out of the cupboard and to use them creatively within the classroom.

For further details about these and other training courses available from Jenny Mosley Consultancies, visit www.circle-time.co.uk

To order a catalogue, please contact:

Positive Press Ltd

28A Gloucester Road, Trowbridge, Wiltshire BA14 0AA

Telephone: 01225 767157 · Fax: 01225 755631 · E-mail: circletime@jennymosley.co.uk

Puppets for Peace

International Puppets for Peace Day is celebrated annually around the world and invites everyone to perform a puppet play about peace. This new movement was influenced by Rudolph Steiner who insisted that the use of puppets has the power to heal the ravages of conflict. Last year, plays were performed in the UK, Canada, USA and South Africa. The belief is that even the simplest tale told through and with puppets will extend a circle of peace which will one day extend and hold everyone within it.

For more information, contact: Suzanne@junipertreepuppets.com